The Gift

fal

fal

Award-winning books from Cornwall

Dear Shadows	DM Thomas
Keeping House	Bill Mycock
Olga's Dreams	Victoria Field
Sleeping in the Rain	St Petrocs
Once in a Blue Moon	Angela Stoner
Seiriol and the Dragon	Michael Power
The Devil and the Floral Dance	DM Thomas
Many Waters	Victoria Field
Prompted to Write	eds Victoria Field & Zeeba Ansari
Knights of Love	Jane Tozer

www.falpublications.co.uk

The Gift

Victoria Field

illustrated by Hannah Cumming

fal

first edition 2007

copyright   text   Victoria Field
             illustrations Hannah Cumming

all rights reserved

ISBN: 978-0-9555661-0-3

published by

Fal Publications
PO Box 74
Truro
TR1 1XS

www.falpublications.co.uk

British Library Cataloguing in Publication Date:
A catalogue record for this book is available from the library.

Printed by

R. Booth Ltd
Antron Hill
Mabe, Cornwall

Author's note: Sipho is pronounced See-po
Acknowledgements:
Our thanks to the staff of University College Falmouth who helped in the preparation of this book.
Thanks to Dawyth Agar for suggesting Sipho's name.

for Melissa and Lucy

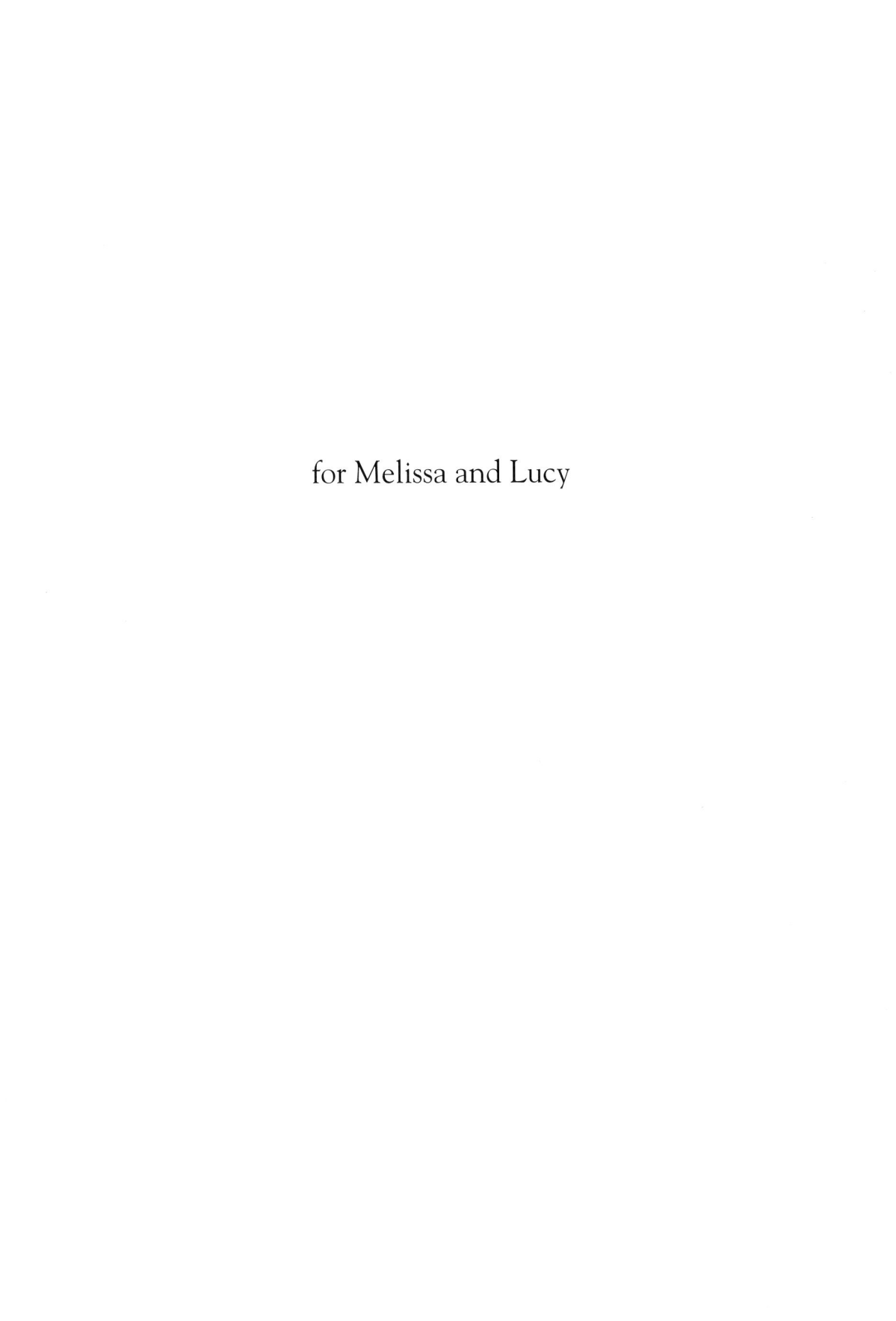

Chapter One

Sipho was exhausted, but he couldn't sleep. He was a long way from home, in a strange bed, in a strange house, in a strange country.

He lay down under the covers, closed his eyes and thought about his mother.

He hadn't seen her for weeks. He had a happy memory of her waving goodbye as he left for school in his brand-new uniform. When he came home, to his horror, his village was full of angry men, smoke and burning houses. Cows and goats were running this way and that. Sipho tried not to think about that terrible sight and instead imagined his mother, happy, waving him off to school.

He felt big wet tears well up under his eyelids. He opened his eyes and stared at the ceiling and willed the tears to disappear. He remembered how his mother used to say, 'Be brave, like a lion.'

Sipho took a deep breath but the tears kept coming.

Suddenly, he felt a soft, wet sensation on his hand. What on earth could that be? He sat up and saw Rusty, a beautiful golden retriever.

In Sipho's country, dogs are not allowed in the house. Rusty, though, was treated like a member of the family. At first Sipho wasn't sure about having a dog in his bedroom , but Rusty looked at him with such kind eyes, he couldn't bear to put her out.

Instead, he got out of bed and looked out of the window and over the city. How cold it looked! And how bright, with street lights and cars going along in the distance. And what on earth was that gigantic building in the middle of the little city?

Sipho looked at Rusty for an answer. Rusty just wagged her tail. And in the morning, Mrs Goody came in to find Sipho fast asleep with Rusty curled up at the foot of the bed.

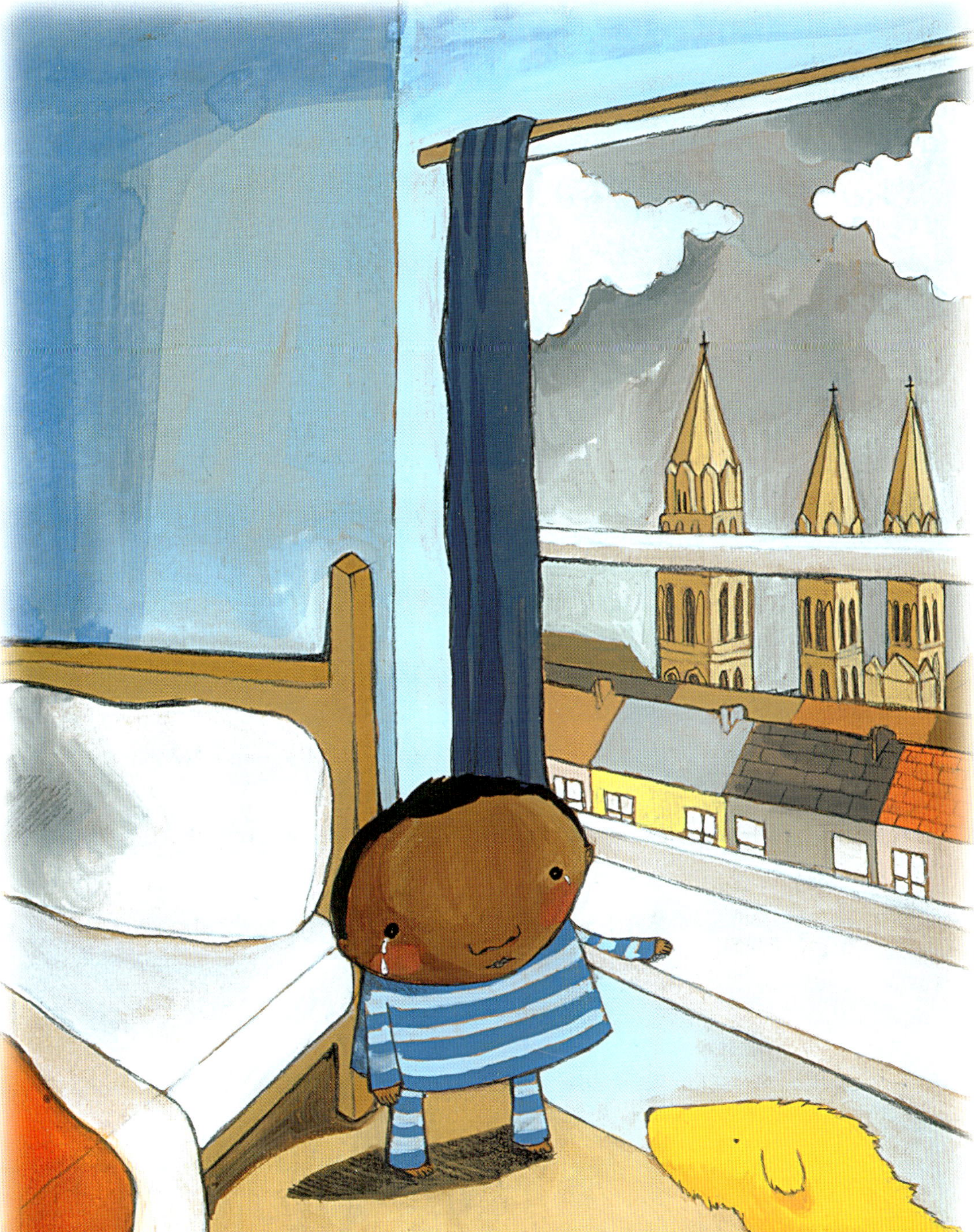

Chapter Two

Mrs Goody was a kind lady and she tried her best to make Sipho feel at home. Sipho couldn't explain that everything was different and that he would *never* feel at home. He was homesick – for food he was used to, for his school friends and most of all for his mother.

One icy-cold winter's day, Mrs Goody took Sipho with her when she went shopping. He waited with her in the bank, in the supermarket and in the library. And then, suddenly, they were standing in front of the gigantic building Sipho had seen from his bedroom window.

It was bigger than he could possibly imagine. He couldn't believe a building could be so tall and so wide. Looking up made Sipho feel dizzy and very small. The more he looked, the more he saw! He couldn't take his eyes off it.

Not only was the building enormous, but it was very complicated. Over the doorway were dozens of figures of men in strange clothes, not to mention angels and animals. He had never seen anything so interesting in his life. Sipho tugged at Mrs Goody's hand to go inside.

'Not now, dear,' she said, 'I've got to get home to put the dinner on.'

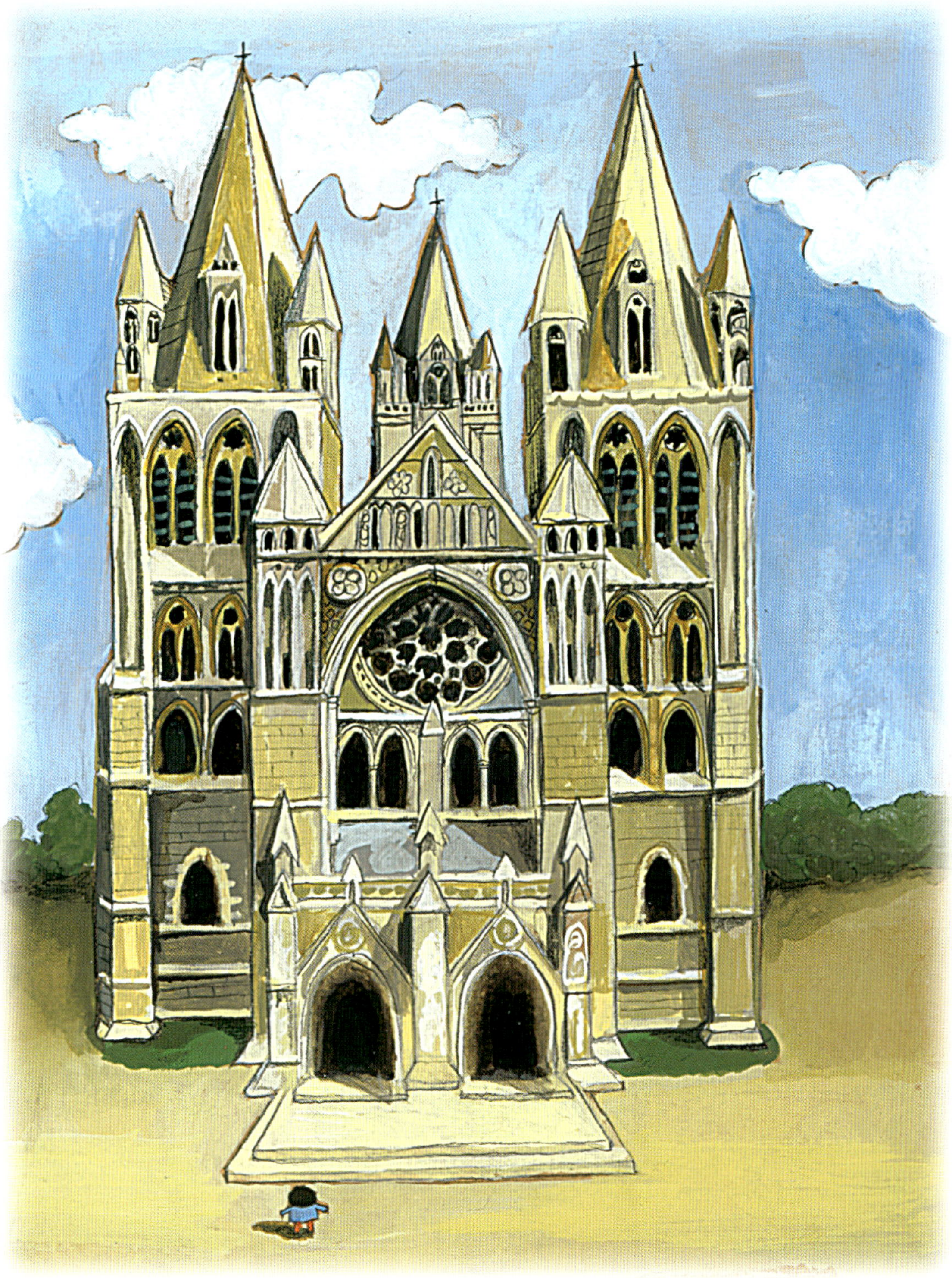

She saw Sipho's disappointed face and added, 'It's the cathedral – a very special building. We'll go in another day, dear.'

Sipho had learned not to argue with grown-ups. He and Mrs Goody walked together around the outside of the building, back to the car park.

The building was so large, it seemed to take an age to pass it. One part was older than the rest, with bricks that were a bit crumbly compared to the splendid grey blocks of the front. On the corner, Sipho saw a carving of a pelican.

A pelican, in this faraway, cold country! Sipho remembered seeing flocks of these great white birds massing in the blue sky over the lakes at home.

As Mrs Goody, hurried him along, he gazed back at the stone carving. The pelican winked at him. Or did it? Sipho sometimes wasn't sure whether he was dreaming or awake.

Chapter Three

One night, the moon was shining so brightly that it was almost like day. Rusty was snoring at the foot of the bed but try as he might, Sipho couldn't get off to sleep.

On a sudden whim, he decided to put on his clothes and go and see the cathedral which had fascinated him so much. He opened the bedroom door quietly and saw that Rusty didn't stir. Sipho then tiptoed down the stairs and out of the front door.

The city was silent. Everyone was sleeping except for the bright moon and the stars which seemed to be smiling down on Sipho as he ran through the empty streets. Soon he found himself in front of the huge building. The great doors were firmly closed with a metal grille in front of them. Sipho slipped through a gate at the side and discovered a tiny door right at the foot of the giant building. Sipho twisted the metal handle and pushed the door with his shoulder. To his surprise, it swung open. He could go inside at last! Sipho tip-toed into the dark space underneath the cathedral. It was full of clutter – old furniture and piles of books. And then, in the murky half-light, he could see two bright yellow eyes staring at him. Sipho stared back.

It was Riff-raff, the cathedral cat. 'Hello,' said Sipho, very nervously. He had hardly spoken since he had arrived in his new country.

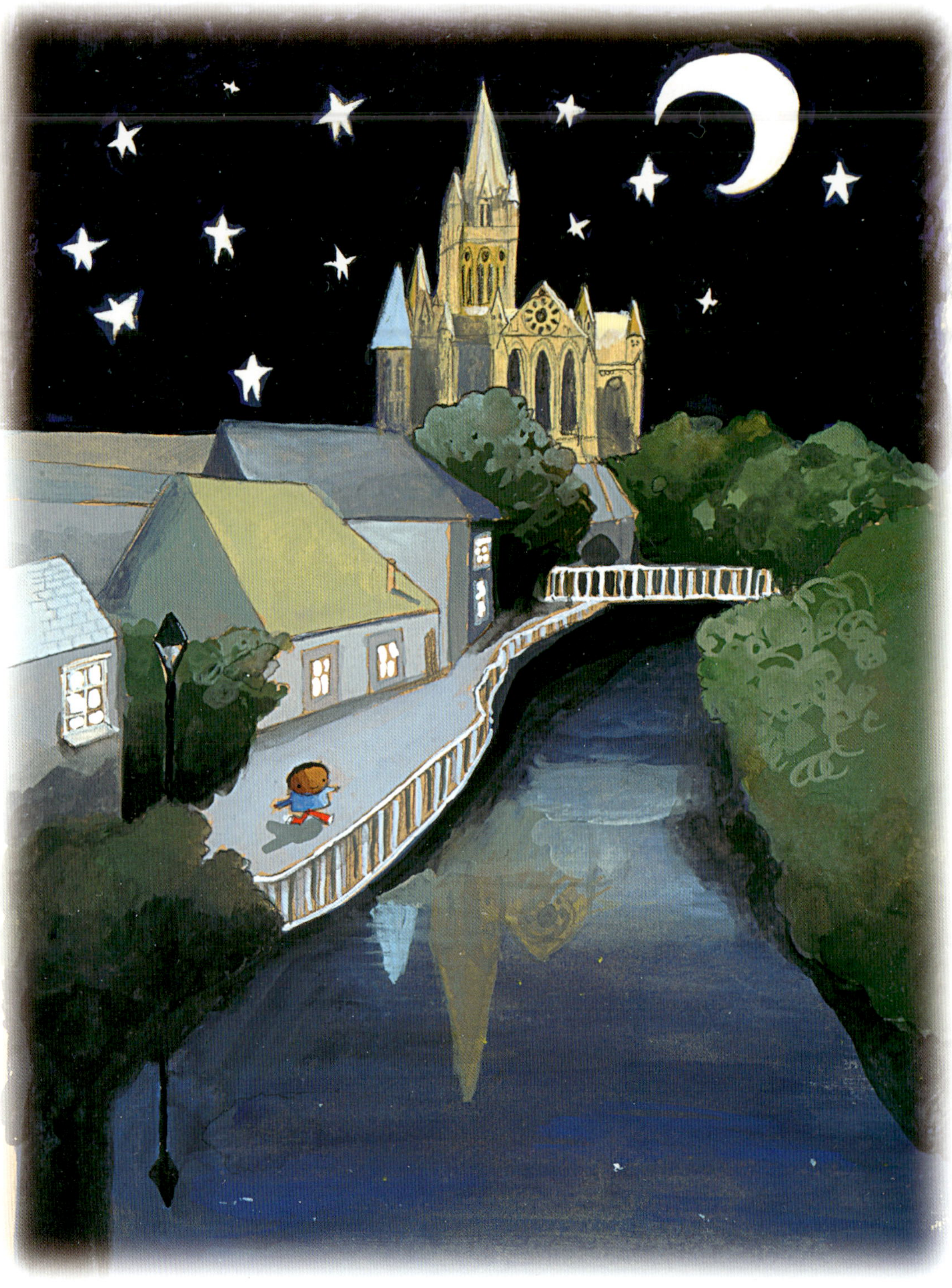

'Hello,' said Riff-raff, 'Would you like me to show you upstairs? It's much more exciting than down here.'

Riff-raff clearly knew his way around. He scampered up some stone steps, opened a small gate and even found some light switches.

Sipho couldn't believe his eyes when he saw the cathedral from the inside. It was vast. Giant stone pillars held up a roof which seemed to be miles away. The pillars were like tree-trunks and the whole building seemed like a magic forest. Everything was very sombre and calm.

Riff-raff rubbed himself against Sipho's legs. 'Come back whenever you like, but best not to say I let you in. I could get into trouble.'

The next morning, Sipho was fast asleep when Mrs Goody came to call him for breakfast. His clothes were in a heap on the floor.

'That's funny,' she thought, 'I'm sure I put them away last night.'

Chapter Four

As the time went by, Sipho became more used to life with Mrs Goody. He managed to eat some of the food she gave him even though it still tasted funny. The days were longer and the sun came out sometimes although he still felt cold. Occasionally, he even smiled but it would never, ever be home.

At night, he often cried himself to sleep and thought about his mother. When she heard him, Rusty would push the bedroom door open with her nose and come and lick his hand.

One night, once again, the moon was extra-bright and, try as he might, Sipho simply couldn't get to sleep. He decided to pay another night-time visit to the cathedral and pulled on his clothes.

This time it was easier to leave the house. He knew which floorboards were creaky and avoided them. He shut the front door carefully so that it made a soft thud rather than a loud click.

After running through the silent streets, he went straight to the little door at the side of the cathedral.

He whispered though the key-hole, 'Riff-raff, Riff-raff, are you there?'

Soon the door swung open and Riff-raff appeared, winding himself up and around Sipho's legs, purring loudly.

'I thought you were never coming back' said Riff-raff, 'I missed you.' Sipho smiled and scratched the cat's head with his fingers. Riff-raff purred even more loudly.

'Come on, let's go upstairs' said Riff-raff and once again scampered up the stone staircase, opening the little gate with a flick of his tail.

Sipho gasped. The cathedral was no longer sombre – there were flowers everywhere. Arrangements of lilies and daffodils and carnations filled the giant building with the scents of the open air. Sipho breathed in deeply and imagined himself at home, walking to school in the sunshine along a track perfumed with wild flowers.

Riff-raff explained that it was almost Easter, the happiest time of the year. After the dark days of winter, everything was coming back to life.

He showed Sipho a very sad painting of Jesus on the cross under a bright pink sky. Sipho noticed that there was a little dog who seemed to be comforting Jesus. 'Hmm' said Riff-raff 'I'm not sure about dogs.'

Then Sipho spotted a statue of a black woman holding a baby. Of course, it was a madonna, a figure of the Virgin Mary, holding the baby Jesus. She had the kindest face he had ever seen and it reminded Sipho of his mother. He picked out some of the lilies from the most magnificent display and laid them carefully on the floor by the black madonna. He said a private prayer that he should see his mother before long.

Riff-raff sat very respectfully and when Sipho had finished he did a little jump, rubbing his head on Sipho's hand.

The next day, one of the vergers, when he came to unlock the cathedral was puzzled by the pile of lilies on the floor. He scratched his head.

Riff-raff said nothing and walked beside the verger looking as innocent as he could.

Chapter Five

Sipho was woken up by the sounds of church bells ringing across the town. At breakfast time, Mrs Goody gave him a huge shiny egg. 'Happy Easter', she said 'Open it up, dear'.

Sipho peeled away the shiny paper to reveal an egg made of chocolate. He nibbled a bit of it – it was delicious. 'Thank you.' he said hesitantly.

Sipho had hardly spoken a word in Mrs Goody's house and to his surprise and consternation, she flung her arms around him and gave him a big wet kiss.

'How lovely to hear your voice, dear. I only wish I could give you back your mum as well as an Easter egg.'

And she hugged and kissed him again. Rusty joined in, nuzzling both of them, with one eye on the chocolate egg.

'Come on, we're going to the cathedral this morning,' said Mrs Goody, moving the egg out of Rusty's reach.

This time, they went into the building at the front, up the steps and through the giant doors. Sipho was amazed to see hundreds of people, all in their best clothes, coming into the building and taking their seats.

When the organ began to play, Sipho jumped out of his skin. He had no idea the pipes could be so loud. Then everyone stood up and started to sing joyfully. Sipho was so used to people being quiet in this cold country, he looked around in amazement.

Just opposite him, he caught the eye of a girl who seemed to be about his own age. She smiled at him and Sipho smiled back.

The service went on for rather a long time. People sat down and stood up and knelt down and queued at the altar. They didn't dance and clap their hands like they do in churches where Sipho came from but everyone looked happy and Sipho felt warm inside.

At one point he saw Riff-raff walk along the choir stalls and then stalk off down the steps into the crypt. The cat didn't look at Sipho and Sipho guessed that he preferred having the cathedral to himself.

After the service had finished, Mrs Goody suggested that they could light a candle for Sipho's mother. She explained it was a way of saying a prayer and that all the flickering candles were prayers going up to heaven.

Sipho lit one carefully, tilting it so that the wick touched the flame of one already lit. He closed his eyes and thought very hard about his mother, hoping that one day he could bury his face in her dress and smell her warm sweet smell as he used to.

When he opened them, he saw that the girl who had smiled at him earlier was standing beside him. She, too, was lighting a candle. Her hand was trembling a little and her eyes were full of tears. Sipho smiled at her and she smiled back.

Chapter Six

When he next visited the cathedral at night, Sipho went straight to the black madonna and said a prayer for his mother. He then went to the picture of the crucifixion and said hello to the little dog – much to Riff-raff's disgust. He also looked for the Noah's Ark window, where there was a giraffe in the stained glass.

On his way to school, he had sometimes seen giraffes, running along in the distance or sometimes nearby, their long rubbery tongues hooking leaves into their mouths.

He was starting to feel at home in the cathedral. Then he saw something that stopped him in his tracks. It was like a picture but it was more real than that. It stood out in 3D and looked as if it could come to life at any moment.

Riff-raff told him the model was made out of terracotta, a kind of baked earth. The model showed scenes of fighting, angry men and soldiers, not with guns but with other weapons and people shouting and panicking. It brought back some terrible memories of when he last saw his mother.

When he came home from school and saw his village burning, Sipho had been whisked away by a kind uncle. He was then passed like a parcel from one place to another until, after a very long frightening journey he had arrived late at night at Mrs Goody's house.

All the memories came pouring into his head and he couldn't stop them. He began to shake and cry. All of a sudden he felt a hand on his shoulder. A hand – not a paw. So it wasn't Riff-raff...

Sipho looked up and to his astonishment, there was the girl from the Easter service.'Don't worry,' she said 'I understand. It's hard to miss someone you love.'

The girl told him how her father had just walked out one night. There had been lots of shouting at home and her mum and dad seemed to argue all the time. She would go to her room and pull the covers over her head but still she could hear raised voices.

She so wanted it to stop and now it was quiet at home. But she missed her dad. The worst thing was her mum wouldn't say where her dad had gone. His shoes were still by the back door as if he might come home any minute.

'What's your name?' she asked.

'Sipho,' said Sipho – 'you say See-po – it means Gift.'

'Oh,' said the girl, 'My name's Lucy – it means Light.'

Riff-raff curled himself around their legs. The less said about his name, the better.

Chapter Seven

Mrs Goody noticed that Sipho seemed happier. Sometimes she even heard him humming as he got dressed . And Sipho did indeed feel a little tiny bit happier. Life is always easier when you have a friend, especially one who understands what you are going through. He imagined telling his mother all about her.

'She's called Lucy and she's exactly my age. She understands how I feel. I can tell her how I miss home, how the food here tastes strange and horrible, how cold it is in this country and how gloomy everything looks. She's kind and funny and she makes me laugh. She's very clever and can draw brilliantly.'

Sipho and Lucy loved exploring the cathedral together at night when there was no one there but Riff-raff.

Sipho showed Lucy all his favourite animals in the building – there are many more than you would think at first sight. The list was getting longer and longer – as well as the pelican on the corner outside, there was the giraffe in the stained glass window, the little dog in the painting, a lamb on the altar front and a huge shiny eagle on the lectern with a sharp beak and talons. There were also the terrified horses in the terracotta relief but Sipho didn't like to look at those.

Lucy loved the flowers best. She showed Sipho the wonderful embroidered tulips with golden thread in the petals. Her favourites though were the three giant windows that were made in the pattern of a rose. So high that only a bird could see the details, the rose windows were just as complicated as a flower with spiralling in patterns and colours. Lucy showed Sipho how the patterns were constructed.

'Look' she said and drew a curve and then another curve meeting it. Sipho was impressed. If only he could make a pencil do such wonderful things!

As summer was coming, the nights were getting shorter and shorter. Riff-raff was very concerned that they shouldn't be caught in the cathedral building. 'Come on,' he said, 'Enough drawing – it's time to go home to your beds!'.

Sipho and Lucy looked at each other and laughed. They would have been happy spending many more hours talking, drawing and just being together. Both of them felt that they had found a 'soul-mate'. A soul-mate is someone who understands you without you having to say a word.

Riff-raff eventually persuaded them to follow him down the stone stairs into the crypt and out of the little door.

But as they came out, someone saw them.

One of the vergers – the people who take care of the cathedral – lived in the house next to the cathedral. He had been woken early by the birds singing and had made himself a cup of tea. As he stood by his bedroom window waiting for the sun to come up, he saw a boy and a girl appear at the little door leading into the crypt, the space under the cathedral where most people never go.

Was he dreaming? He rubbed his eyes hard and when he opened them again, Sipho and Lucy had disappeared.

So many extraordinary things that happen every day in the cathedral, he didn't always know what was real.

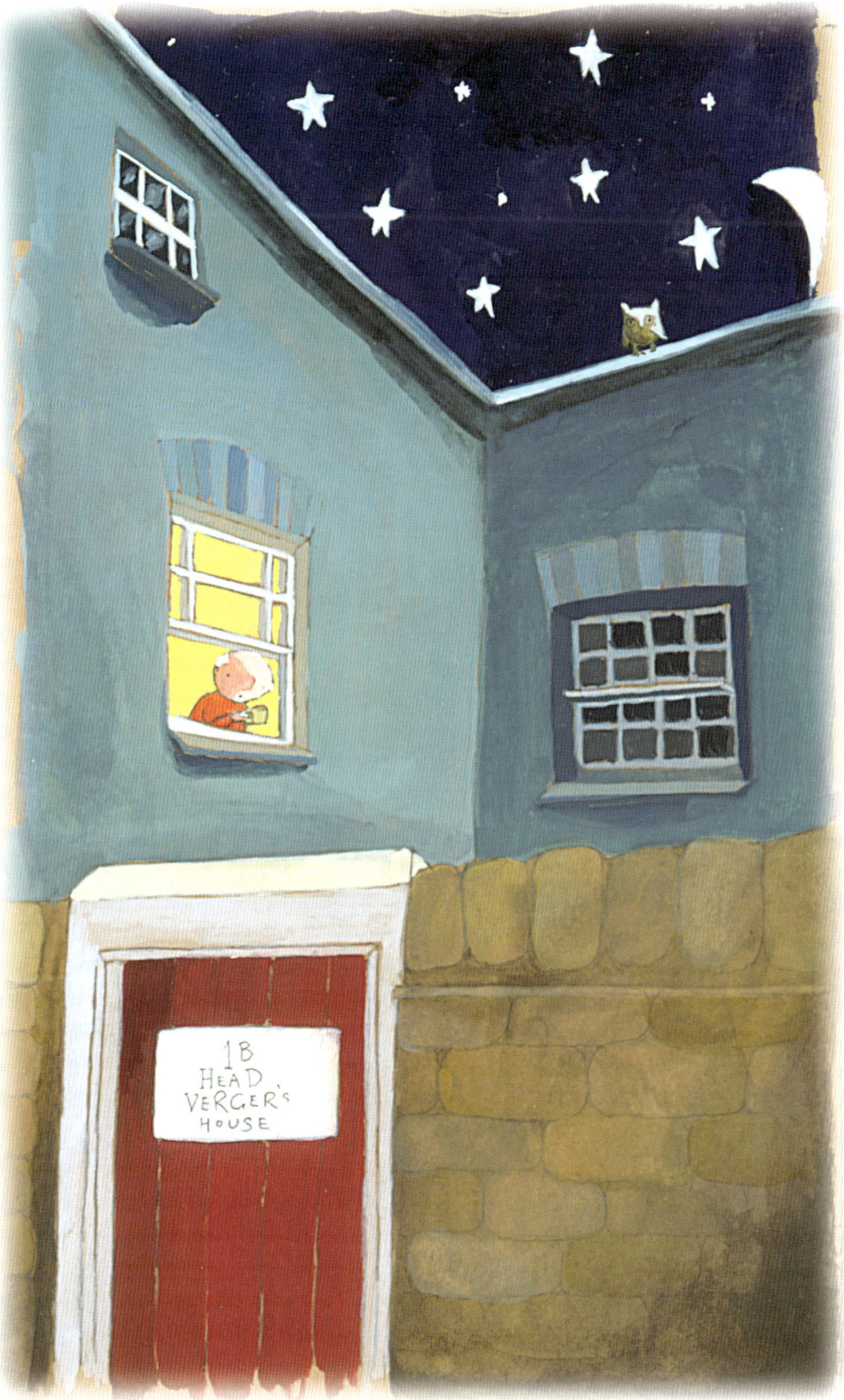
1B
HEAD
VERGER's
HOUSE

Chapter Eight

When summer came, it was even more difficult to sleep. Sipho had lost track of the days but he knew it was more than six months since he had last seen his mother.

Her last words to him were 'Run, Sipho, run – don't worry, I'll come and find you. Be brave!'.

But she hadn't come to find him, and here he was in a strange country, wondering what had happened to her and fearing the worst.

Rusty always sensed when Sipho was especially sad and she stood wagging her tail against the bed. Thump, thump, thump. Eventually, Sipho smiled through his tears and stroked her head. Thump, thump, thump – Rusty's tail bumped even more quickly against the bed.

Sipho once again decided to go to the cathedral, hoping he would find Lucy.

When Riff-raff let him in, Lucy was already there, waiting for him in the crypt.

'I was hoping you would come,' she said. 'I've got an idea.'

The idea was terrifying to Sipho. Lucy had found a secret staircase that would take them up through the giant building, into the roof-space and eventually out onto the roof itself.

Sipho and Riff-raff weren't sure but Lucy was very determined. 'Come on,' she said, 'It's a beautiful night. Please!'

Sipho remembered his mother telling him to be brave and, even though his heart was beating like a drum, he followed Lucy up the narrow winding staircase.

It went on and on and up and up. Sipho was beginning to feel dizzy. Lucy ran on ahead, laughing with excitement.

Suddenly, the staircase ran out and they found themselves at the top of one of the spires. 'Go on, have a look out,' said Lucy.

Sipho very tentatively swung his legs over the side of the window ledge and exclaimed 'Oh my goodness – it is so high!' He gripped hold of Riff-raff so tightly the cat squeaked in protest.

Then Lucy had another idea. 'Let's take off and fly!' By now Sipho had realised he couldn't refuse Lucy anything. But flying – that was impossible.

A moment later, they were airborne. Sipho held Lucy's hand with one hand and Riff-raff's paw with the other. He was terrified and exhilarated all at once. The world looked spectacular.

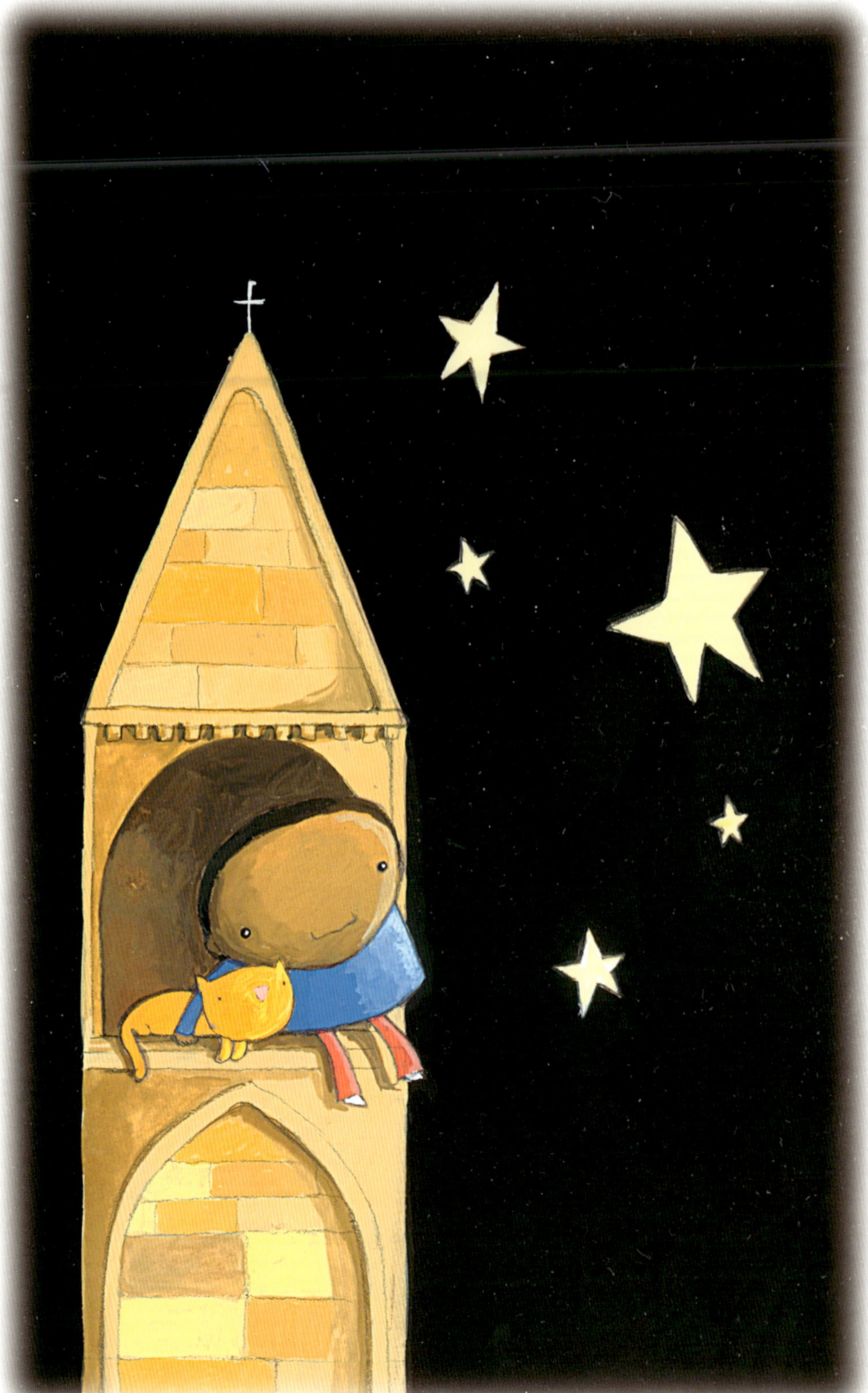

He could see green fields and high moorland, little houses and roads like ribbons. And all around the sea, blue and grey and green.

He smiled at Lucy and she gave him a lovely smile back. He smiled at Riff-raff and even above the loud rushing of air in his ears, he could hear the faint rumble of his purr.

'It's beautiful!' Sipho shouted 'The world looks so beautiful from up here!'

And so Sipho, Lucy and Riff-raff spent the next few hours, swooping above the countryside, diving in and out of white clouds, shouting and laughing with excitement and sheer love of life.

'You see,' shouted Lucy as they flew high above the cathedral, 'Everything's possible!'

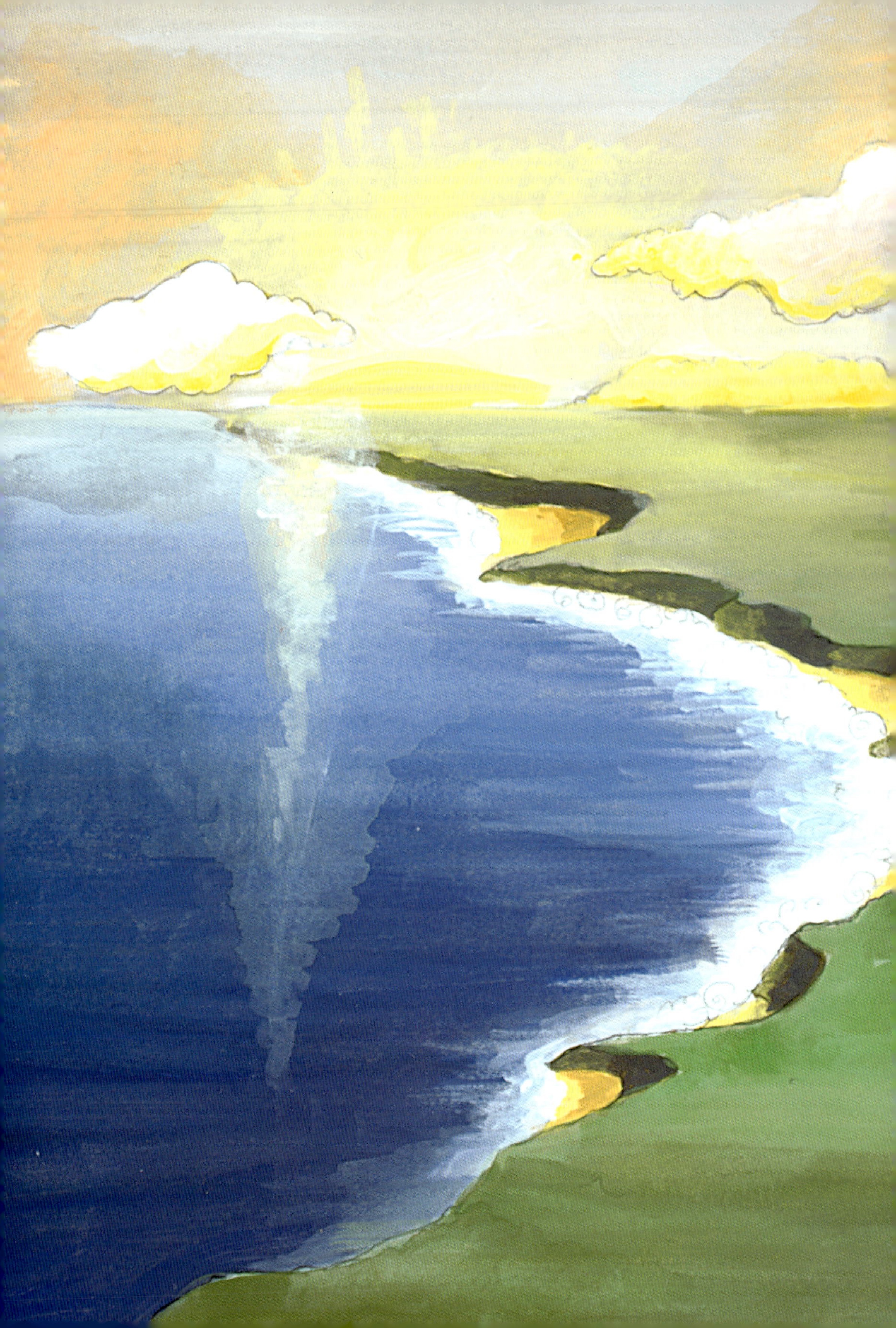

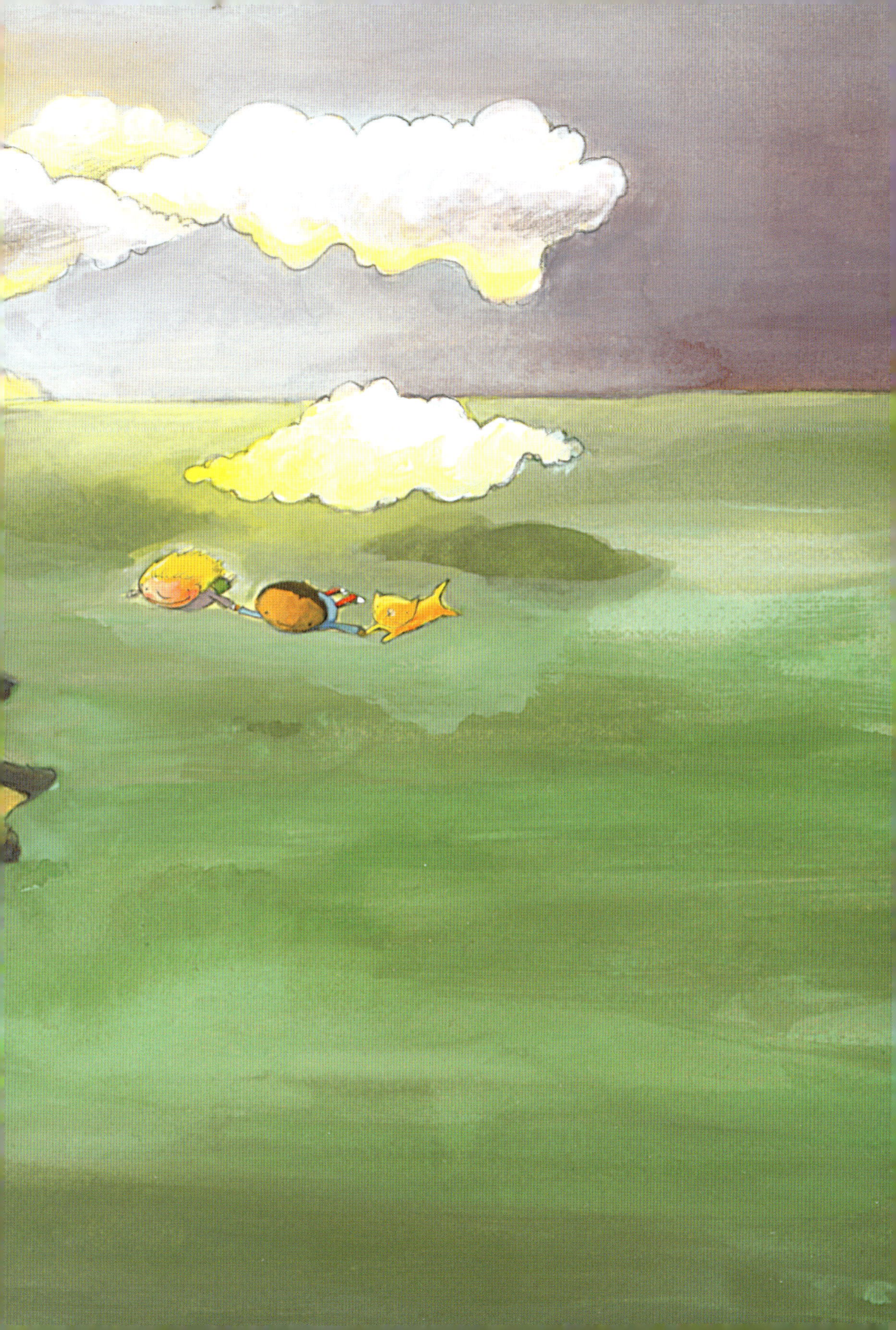

Chapter Nine

After their adventures, Sipho, Lucy and Riff-raff were exhausted and fell into a deep sleep.

They had snuggled up together down in the crypt, still laughing and giggling about the excitement of flying high in the sky. One by one, they had started to yawn.

First, Riff-raff's eyelids closed and he fell into a deep slumber. Lucy's head began to nod and soon she was asleep, snoring very gently. Sipho thought to himself, we must remember to go home before it's light. But then he, too, felt drowsy. 'I'll just close my eyes for a second,' he thought. But immediately, he was deep into a dreamless sleep.

****

'WELL, I NEVER! WHAT HAVE WE GOT HERE?'

A big booming voice woke the three of them up all at once.

Peering down at them was one of the vergers who had just arrived to unlock the cathedral.

'How on earth did you get in here? And what *have* you been up to?' he shouted, shaking his head.

Riff-raff stood up, stretched slowly and elegantly and walked away through the crypt, looking as innocent as can be.

Lucy and Sipho sat wide-eyed, unable to say a word. Lucy's eyes began to brim with tears and Sipho's bottom lip began to tremble.

The verger looked less stern. 'The dear of 'em,' he said to himself, 'Poor little angels.'

'Now, my handsomes, you come with me and we'll see if we can find out where you both live. Your mums and dads are going to be very worried.'

Lucy's eyes brimmed even more and Sipho couldn't control his trembling lip.

Chapter Ten

Mrs Goody was very, very cross. She kept repeating that Sipho was her responsibility and that he had been very, very naughty. He was a *big* responsibility and it was *very* irresponsible of him to go wandering around the city at night.

She even seemed to be cross with Rusty. When the dog came to lick Sipho's hand, Mrs Goody wagged her finger and snapped, 'Basket, Rusty!' and the puzzled dog slunk away to the corner of the kitchen.

She sat Sipho in a chair and talked to him for so long he nearly fell asleep again. The same words wandered in and out of his ears – responsibility, naughty, irresponsible, BIG responsibility …

And all the time he was remembering flying over the cathedral, hand-in-hand – or hand-in-paw – with his friends. He couldn't help himself and a little smile passed over his face.

Mrs Goody was furious. 'This isn't funny! You have been very naughty.' Rusty lay watching them, one eye open and one eye closed.

It seemed his night-time excursions were definitely at an end. Mrs Goody put an extra lock on the front door and hid the key. She checked that Sipho was in his room several times a night.

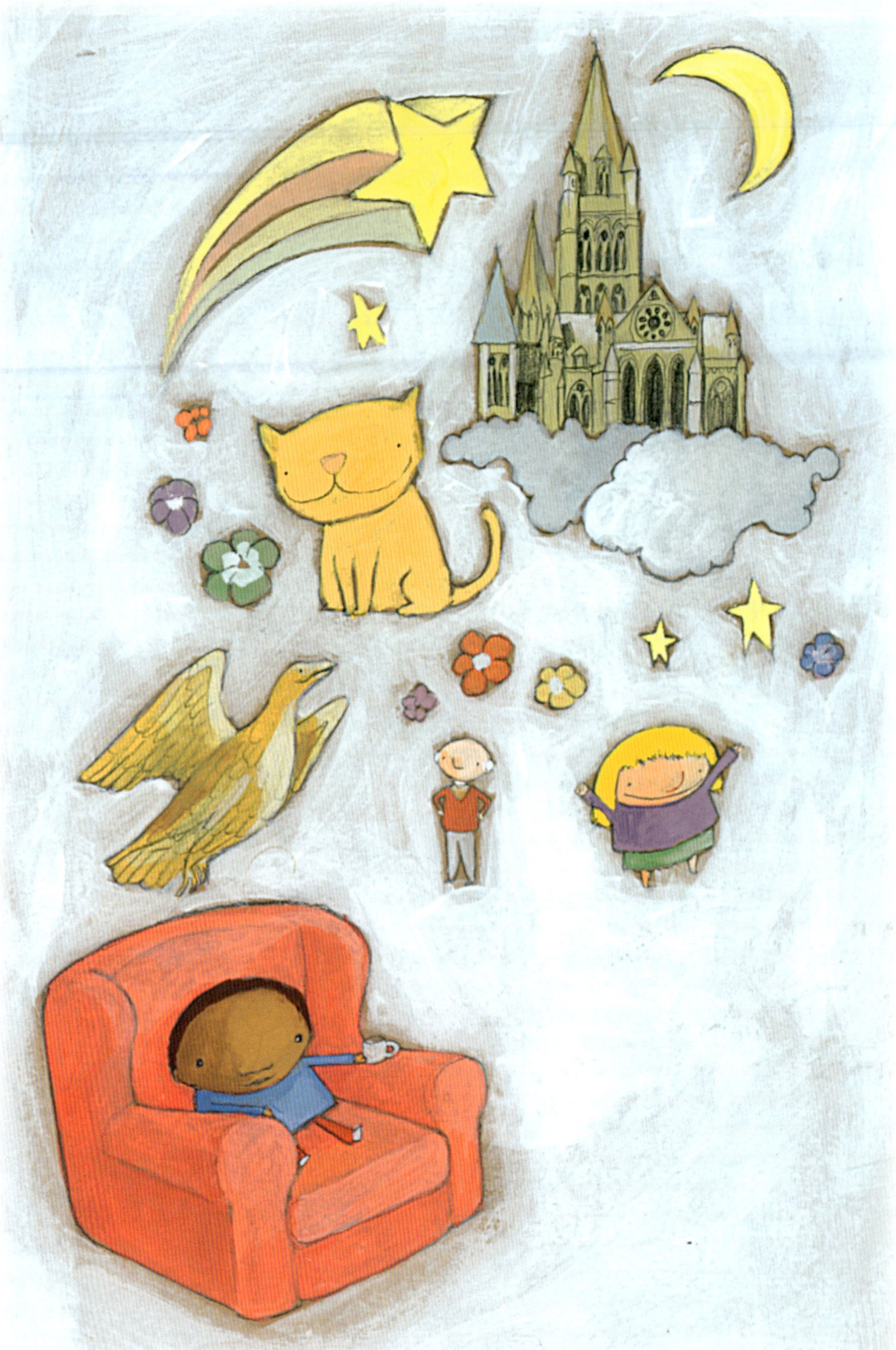

During the day, Sipho sat sadly in a chair and thought about the cathedral and his friends. He wanted to stroke Riff-raff's head and hear him purr. He wanted to draw the rose windows with Lucy. More than anything, he wanted to take off from the spire and fly high in the sky. Sipho sank into the chair and sighed deeply.

After a week or so, Mrs Goody stopped being cross and became kind again.

'I'm sorry to be so strict, dear,' she said, 'It's just that you are a big responsibility ...'

Chapter Eleven

The days turned into weeks and the weeks turned into months and still Sipho hadn't been back to the cathedral.

Now, he was missing Lucy and Riff-raff as well as his mother. It was a different kind of missing. Missing his friends was like a heavy stone in his chest, whereas missing his mother was a sharp pain that pricked him behind the eyes.

The days were beginning to get darker and colder again. Sipho was feeling particularly gloomy one day when Mrs Goody told him that Christmas was coming and they would once again be visiting the cathedral.

Everything became more lively and colourful. Sipho drove with Mrs Goody to a farm outside the city where they chose a tree from dozens piled up in a barn. The tree made the car smell delicious, like a forest.

When they got home, Mrs Goody went up into her attic and passed down cardboard boxes, full of tinsel and baubles and fairy lights. Together they decorated the tree in the front room and at night, it sparkled in the window, like the stars did outside.

When they went shopping together, Sipho heard people singing carols in the street, there was music in the shops and decorations everywhere. 'Happy Christmas' people would say to each other.

Mrs Goody explained that Christmas was a time for giving – just as God had given his most precious thing, his only son, as a little baby, to people on earth.

She asked Sipho what he would like for Christmas and what he would like to give as a present.

Sipho said he would like to buy a squeaky toy bone for Rusty to play with and some very special pencils for Lucy.

'And what would *you* like for Christmas, dear?' asked Mrs Goody.

Sipho thought of his mother's smiling face but couldn't say a word.

Mrs Goody gave him a hug and said, 'You never know, dear. Dreams do come true.'

On Christmas morning, Sipho prayed hard that he might see his mother – it would be the best Christmas present in the world. At the foot of his bed was a stocking with all kinds of good things in it – an orange, a bag of nuts, a picture book of the cathedral and a warm hat and scarf .

Sipho said thank you to Mrs Goody but he found it hard to hide his disappointment. After Christmas Dinner – which even Sipho admitted was delicious – he gave Mrs Goody a present. It was a beautiful drawing of the cathedral's rose windows which Sipho had done all by himself, remembering the instructions from Lucy.

Mrs Goody said thank you and gave him another hug and a knowing smile.

Then Sipho gave Rusty her squeaky toy bone. She wagged her tail in delight and the three of them spent the next hour out in the cold garden throwing it for her to fetch.

Sipho still longed for the best present of all.

'I have a treat for you,' said Mrs Goody. 'Tomorrow is the Service for Pets at the cathedral. We'll be able to take Rusty with us and she can meet all the other animals.'

Sipho was delighted. He would see Lucy and Riff-raff, his very best friends.

Chapter Twelve

The cathedral was packed. Every row of chairs not only had grown-ups and children of all ages but every animal you could think of.

... Mrs and Mrs Parker had brought their python. The Carter family were all sitting with their cats on their shoulders. Graham had brought his guinea pig, Eliza had her lizard. Oliver had an owl on his knee, Matilda, her mouse in a cage on the seat beside her. Jenny brought her gerbils, Hannah, her hamster, Belinda, her budgerigar and right in the middle of the front row was a boy called Ian with his pet iguana.

There were dogs galore and Rusty was delighted. She wagged her tail at every dog she saw, from little Jack Russells to giant Great Danes. Sipho felt proud to be with Rusty – she was so beautiful and so friendly.

Mrs Goody suggested that they sat in the middle of the cathedral so they could see all the animals and hear everything that was going on. Sipho spotted Lucy and her mum and waved. Lucy gave a little jump for joy and waved back.

'Thank you for the pencils,' she mouthed over the hubbub of barking dogs and chattering children.

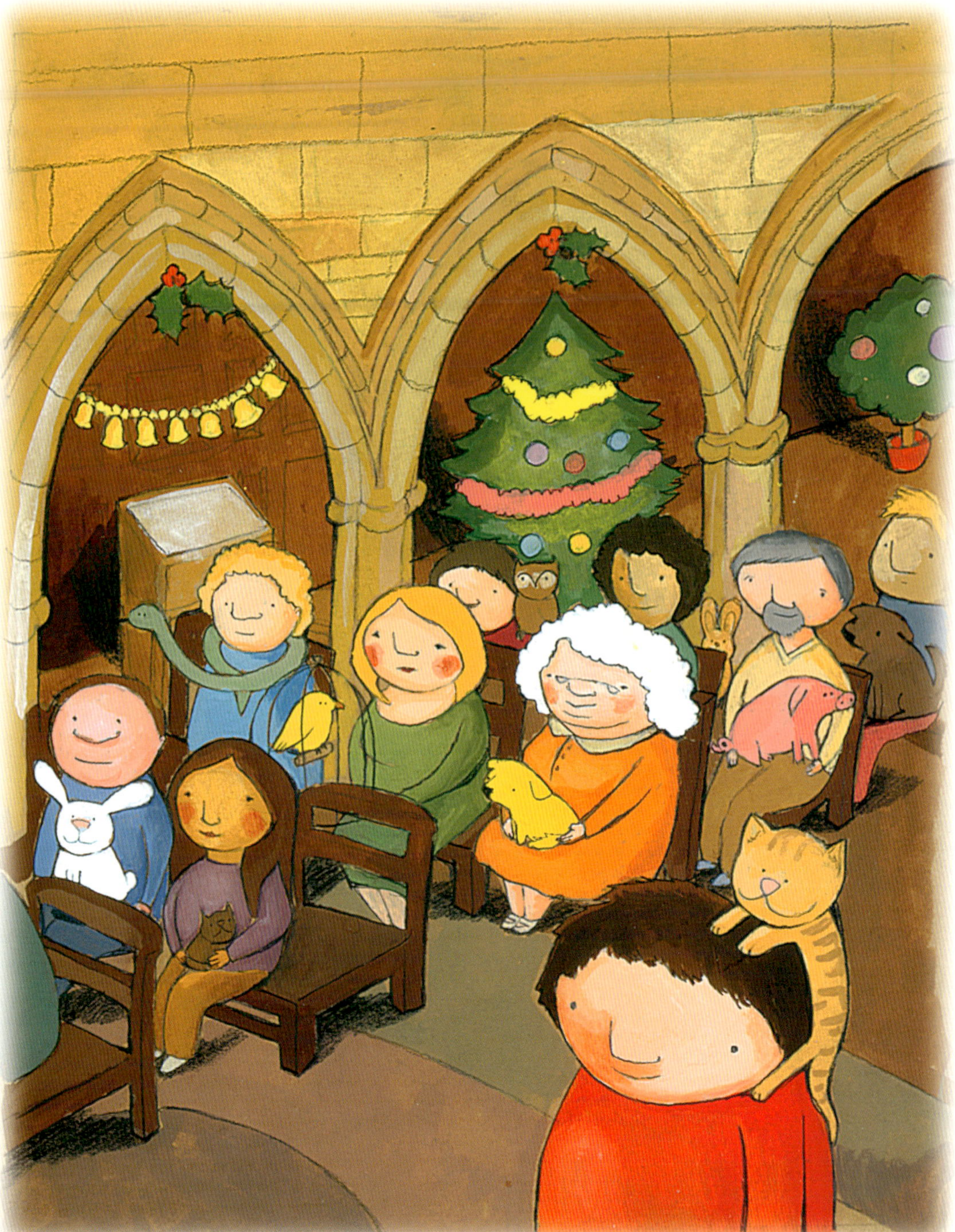

'You're welcome,' Sipho mouthed back.

The verger who had found Sipho and Lucy walked past with Riff-raff beside him. He tousled Sipho's hair and said 'Special day for you, my handsome.' Sipho wondered what he meant.

Riff-raff rubbed himself on Sipho's legs and did his special little jump. He didn't say a word but as he followed the verger along the aisle, he turned and gave Sipho a big wink.

The service was chaotic and wonderful. They all sang carols at the tops of their voices and the dogs joined in, howling and yapping.

Then, all the animals and their humans processed around the building, past the Christmas tree, the enormous crib with its model of the stable where Jesus was born and up to the high altar with its flickering candles. Sipho, Mrs Goody and Rusty were squashed against a man carrying a giant rabbit and a donkey with a little girl dressed as Mary on its back.

They sang another carol and said some prayers, giving thanks for creation and all the animals.

Chapter 13

As they turned to leave the cathedral after the service, Sipho suddenly felt very strange.

At the far end, near the giant west doors, he could see a figure that was familiar, standing next to a man he didn't know.

'I'm dreaming,' he said to himself, 'it can't be true.'

He looked up at Mrs Goody and she nodded. 'Yes, dear, it *is* true.'

He looked down at Rusty who wagged her tail harder than he'd ever seen before. Riff-raff rubbed himself on Sipho's legs, purring like an engine.

The cathedral fell silent and Sipho felt the eyes of all the people and all the animals, looking first at him and then at the two figures at the far end of the building.

Sipho's heart was beating like a drum and his legs felt rooted to the spot. Then he heard Lucy give a cry of delight. 'My daddy!'

The verger gave Sipho a little push 'There you go, lad, happy Christmas!'

She had kept her promise – she had come for him!

And Sipho ran, ran, ran, as fast as he could, so fast that it felt like flying, flying over the whole beautiful planet, and flung himself into the arms of his mother.

The best gift of all.

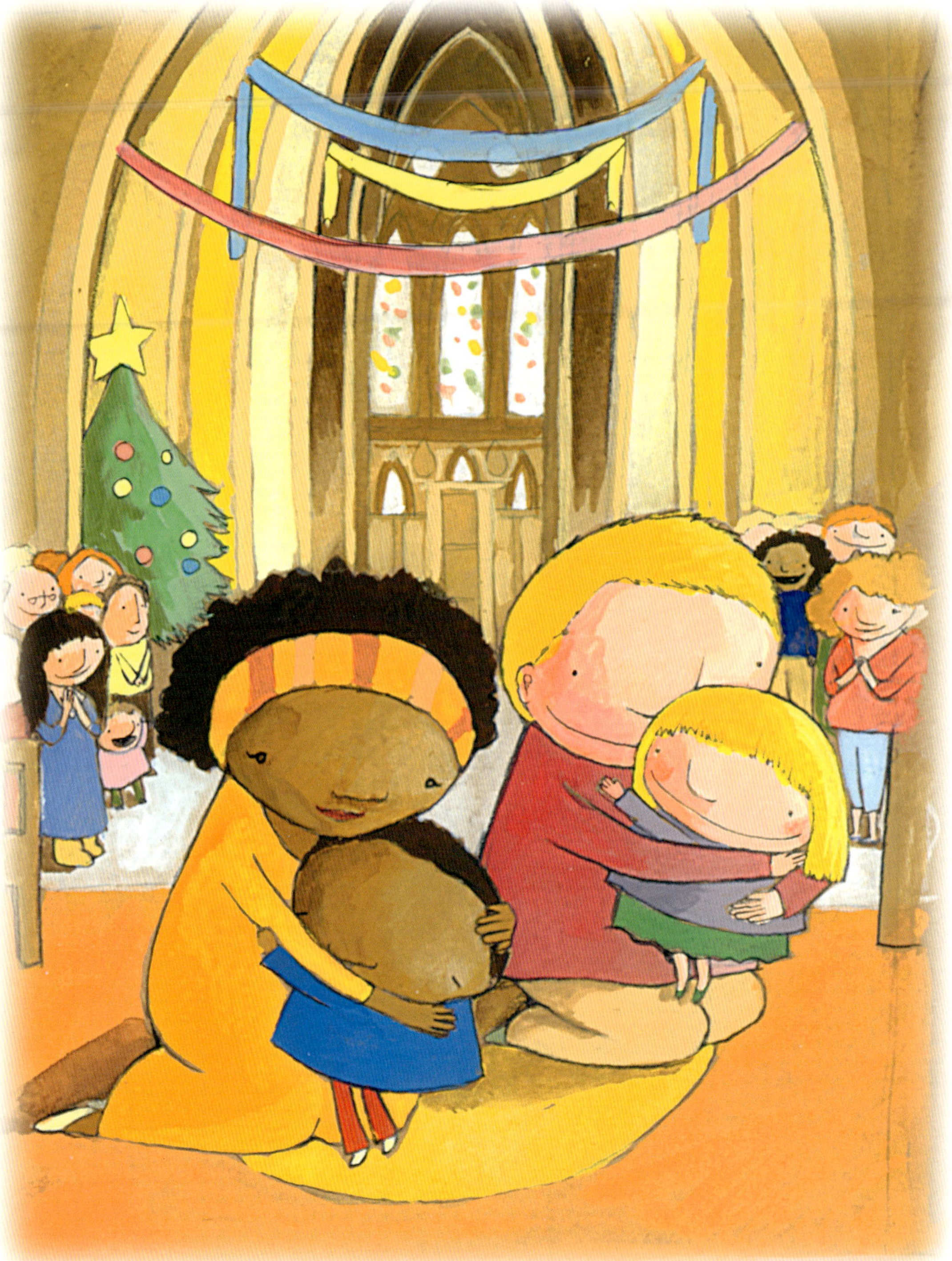

Victoria Field is a writer and poetry therapist based in Cornwall. She has two collections of poetry, *Olga's Dreams* and *Many Waters*, both from fal, the latter based on her writing residency at Truro Cathedral. She has co-edited two books on therapeutic writing and Hall for Cornwall have produced two of her plays. This is her first children's book.

Hannah Cumming studied Illustration at University College Falmouth, and graduated in 2007 with first class honours. Her work has been exhibited in Falmouth and London, and twice been Highly Commended in the Macmillan Children's Book Prize. For further information please visit www.hannahillustration.com